The Texas Revolution

Fighting for Independence

Kelly Rodgers

Consultant

Julie Hyman, MS.Ed.
Social Studies Coordinator
Birdville ISD

Publishing Credits

Dona Herweck Rice, *Editor-in-Chief*
Lee Aucoin, *Creative Director*
Marcus McArthur, Ph.D., *Associate Education Editor*
Neri Garcia, *Senior Designer*
Stephanie Reid, *Photo Editor*
Rachelle Cracchiolo, M.S.Ed., *Publisher*

Image Credits:

Cover, p.1 LOC [LC–USZ62–21489]; pp.2–3 LOC [LC-USZC4–2133]; p.4 (top) North Wind Picture Archives; p.5 DeGolyer Library; p.6 State Preservation Board, Austin, Texas; p.7 (top) Carolina Digital Library & Archives; p.8 The Granger Collection; p.9 North Wind Picture Archives; p.10 Tip. de J. R. Navarro (1850), via. Google Books; p.11 The Lawbook Exchange, Ltd., Clark, NJ.; p.12 Texas State Library & Archives Commission; p.13 LOC [LC–USZ62–21276]; p.14, 15 Gonzales Memorial Museum; p.16 Star of the Republic Museum; p.17 Corbis; p.18 Houston, Andrew Jackson (1938), UNT Libraries, Denton, Texas; p.19 (sidebar) Bridgeman Art Library; p.21 (top) Corbis, (bottom) State Preservation Board, Austin, Texas; p.22 The Granger Collection; p.23 Bridgeman Art Library, (sidebar) State Preservation Board, Austin, Texas; p.24 Alamy; p.25 (top) A Pictorial History of Texas (1885), (bottom) Bridgeman Art Library; p.26 Bridgeman Art Library; p.27 State Preservation Board, Austin, Texas; p.28 LOC [LOC_61365bs]; p.29 North Wind Picture Archives; p.32 Gonzales Memorial Museum; All other images Shutterstock.

Teacher Created Materials
5301 Oceanus Drive
Huntington Beach, CA 92649-1030
http://www.tcmpub.com

ISBN 978-1-4333-5046-7

Table of Contents

Transitions in Texas 4–5

Causes of the Revolution 6–13

The Revolution Begins 14–19

The Alamo 20–23

Declaring Independence 24–27

An Independent State 28–29

Glossary.. 30

Index.. 31

Your Turn! 32

Transitions in Texas

Most states had easy **transitions** from **colonies** to statehood, but the story of Texas is much more complex. Texas changed hands many times. American Indians, Spain, France, Mexico, the Republic of Texas, the Confederate States of America, and the United States have all claimed Texas at some point in time.

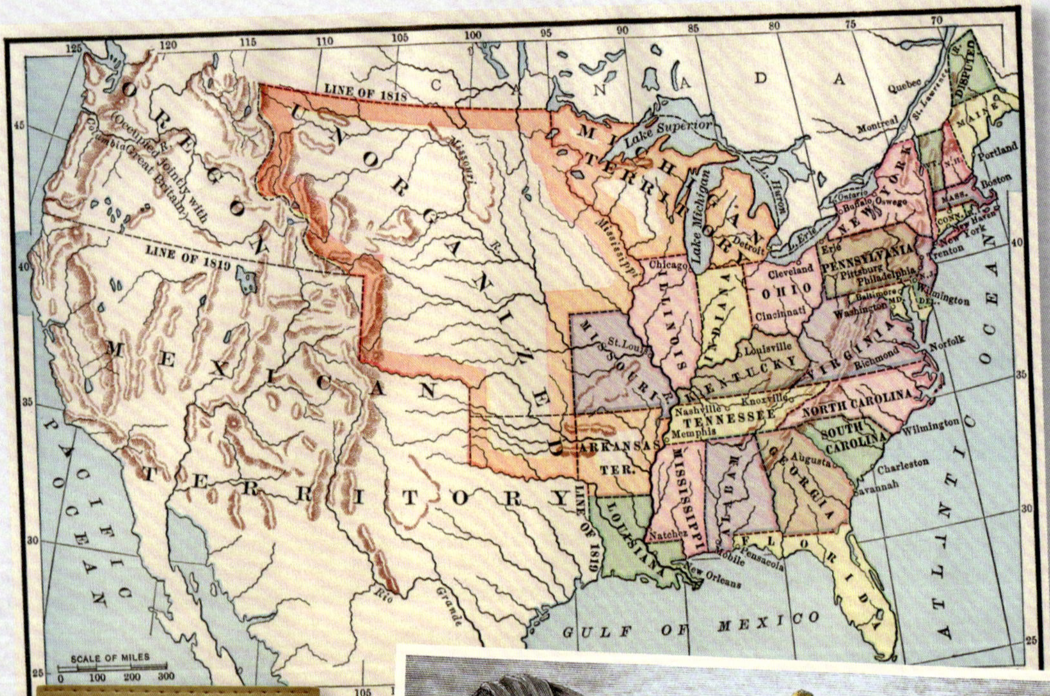

map of Mexican and U.S. territory, 1830

settlers moving west

In 1821, the people of New Spain won their independence, or freedom. They called their new nation *Mexico*. Mexico was a poor country from the start. The northern part of the country, known as *Tejas* (TAY-has), or Texas, was hard to defend, so Mexico invited people from the United States to move there. Soon, there were more American settlers than Mexican-born people in Texas.

Antonio López de Santa Anna

In 1833, Antonio López de Santa Anna (ahn-TOH-nee-oh LOH-pehs deh SAHN-tah AH-nah) was elected President of Mexico. Santa Anna wanted more control for himself and his government. He did not want the **provinces** to be powerful, and he wanted to end **immigration**. He made new, strict laws for the people of Texas. Tensions between Santa Anna and Texans grew. This led to the Texas **Revolution**.

Religion, Independence, and Unity

Mexican Independence was achieved through an agreement called the *Plan of Iguala* (ee-WAHL-uh), or the *Plan of the Three Guarantees*. Under the plan, the Roman Catholic Church would unify Mexico. Mexico would be an independent state, and all people would be equal.

Tejanos, Texians, and Texans

During the time of the Texas Revolution, the people of Texas were known by several names. Those who were Mexican-born were known as **Tejanos** (tay-HA-noz). People living in Texas but born in the United States were called **Texians** (TEK-see-uhnz). The word *Texans* meant anyone who lived in Texas, regardless of their home country.

Causes of the Revolution

The Empresarios

Moses Austin was once a wealthy businessman and banker, but he lost most of his money in the Panic of 1819. He thought he could regain his wealth if he moved to Texas. Spain granted Austin permission to **recruit** 300 American families to settle on 200,000 acres of Texas land.

Stephen F. Austin with his colonists in 1824

Moses Austin died before he was able to go to Texas. His son, Stephen F. Austin, carried out his father's plan. In January 1822, Austin went to Texas to set up a new colony.

It did not take long for Austin to find families willing to move to Texas. The land was perfect for a cotton **plantation** system like the one in the American South.

Settlers arrive in Texas.

Austin's colony was very successful. Soon, other Americans applied for land grants in Texas. These men were called ***empresarios*** (im-press-AHR-ee-ohz). This means "businessmen" in Spanish. The empresario's job was to get families to settle in Texas. Each empresario received a certain amount of land for a set number of families. During the 1820s, the empresarios brought thousands of settlers to Texas.

cotton plant

Panic of 1819

In 1819, the United States faced a financial crisis. Cotton prices fell quickly. People had a hard time getting loans to run their businesses and farms. Many Americans lost their jobs and homes. The economy did not recover until 1823.

The De León Colony

Martin De León (mahr-TEEN deh leh-OHN) was a Mexican **rancher**. He passed through Texas while driving his mules to market in New Orleans. When De León saw the **thriving** grasslands, he decided to make a new start there. By 1824, De León and 12 Mexican families had moved to Texas. Over time, other families joined them.

The Republic of Fredonia

Empresario Haden Edwards heightened tensions between the settlers and the Mexican government. In 1826, he tried to **secede** (si-SEED) from Mexico. He wanted to form his own independent Republic of Fredonia (freh-DOH-nee-uh). Austin and many colonists sided with the Mexican government. The **rebellion** was put down. But the Mexican government began to distrust the colonists.

American Indians in Texas

As American Indian tribes in the American South lost their territory, they immigrated to Texas. The American settlers who moved to Texas developed different relationships with the tribes. Some relationships were good, while others resulted in violence.

Tensions in Texas

Sometimes, two or more colonists claimed to have the rights to the same plot of land. Colonists began to have many conflicts with Mexico about their rights. Mexico's government knew that some American leaders wanted to make Texas part of the United States. All of these problems led to tensions in Texas.

There were also conflicts between Tejanos and Texians. Tejanos wanted Texas to be successful. They understood that the Texians played an important role in the state's success. But they were worried that they were losing control of their land.

Comanche on the attack

By 1830, nearly 10,000 Americans had settled in Texas. Many of them ignored the Mexican requirement that they become Catholic. And some of them brought slaves to Texas to work on their farms and plantations. Slavery was not illegal in Texas. But the Mexican government wanted to end the practice.

slaves picking cotton

There also were problems with the American Indians who lived in Texas. Many were willing to live peacefully with the new immigrants. But others were not. The colonists, including Austin, viewed some tribes as enemies. Soon, violent conflicts broke out between Texans and American Indians.

The Law of April 6, 1830

Mexican General Manuel de Mier y Terán

By 1828, Mexican leaders had grown concerned about their loss of control in Texas. Mexico wanted to find out how they could keep Texas from being taken over by Americans. They sent General Manuel de Mier y Terán (mee-YEHR ee teh-RAHN) on an **inspection** tour.

Mier y Terán was worried about what he found. Tejanos told him that they thought the Texians were planning to fight against Mexican rule. Most of the Tejanos who had settled in Texas were poor and uneducated. Many Texians felt superior to the Tejanos. The Texians wanted to separate Texas from the Mexican state of Coahuila (kaw-ah-WEE-lah) and start their own state.

Mier y Terán returned from the tour in January 1829. He reported that the situation was dangerous. He said that it would be a big mistake to separate Coahuila and Texas into two states.

It was not until April 6, 1830, that the government took action by passing a new law. The Law of April 6, 1830 made most Texans angry. It banned American immigration into Texas. It also put an end to empresario contracts. It stated that slaves could not be brought into Texas. It also forced Texans to pay taxes on goods shipped into and out of Texas. Many Texians and some Tejanos felt the new law took away too many of their freedoms. They wanted the right to make their own laws.

INICIATIVA DE LEY PROPONIENDO AL GOBIERNO LAS MEDIDAS QUE SE DEBIAN TOMAR PARA LA SEGURIDAD DEL ESTADO DE

TEJAS

Y CONSERVAR la INTEGRIDAD DEL TERRITORIO MEXICANO de cuyo proyecto emanó la ley de 6 abril de 1830.

Lúcas Alaman

Biblioteca Aportación Histórica
Editor Vargas Rea
México 1946

the Law of April 6, 1830

Mier y Terán

Mier y Terán was a smart man. He had helped Mexico win independence from Spain. During the 1820s, he held many different government jobs. He was a Mexican patriot who wanted what was best for Mexico.

Lucas Alaman

Lucas Alaman was an important Mexican leader. Among other things, he was in charge of foreign affairs. He was alarmed when Mier y Terán told him about the situation in Texas. Alaman was worried that Texas would join the United States. He hoped the Law of April 6, 1830 would keep Texas firmly under Mexican control.

Revolutionary Rumblings

The Texans were upset with the Mexican government. Arguments over slaves and taxes continued. At times, the arguments turned to violence.

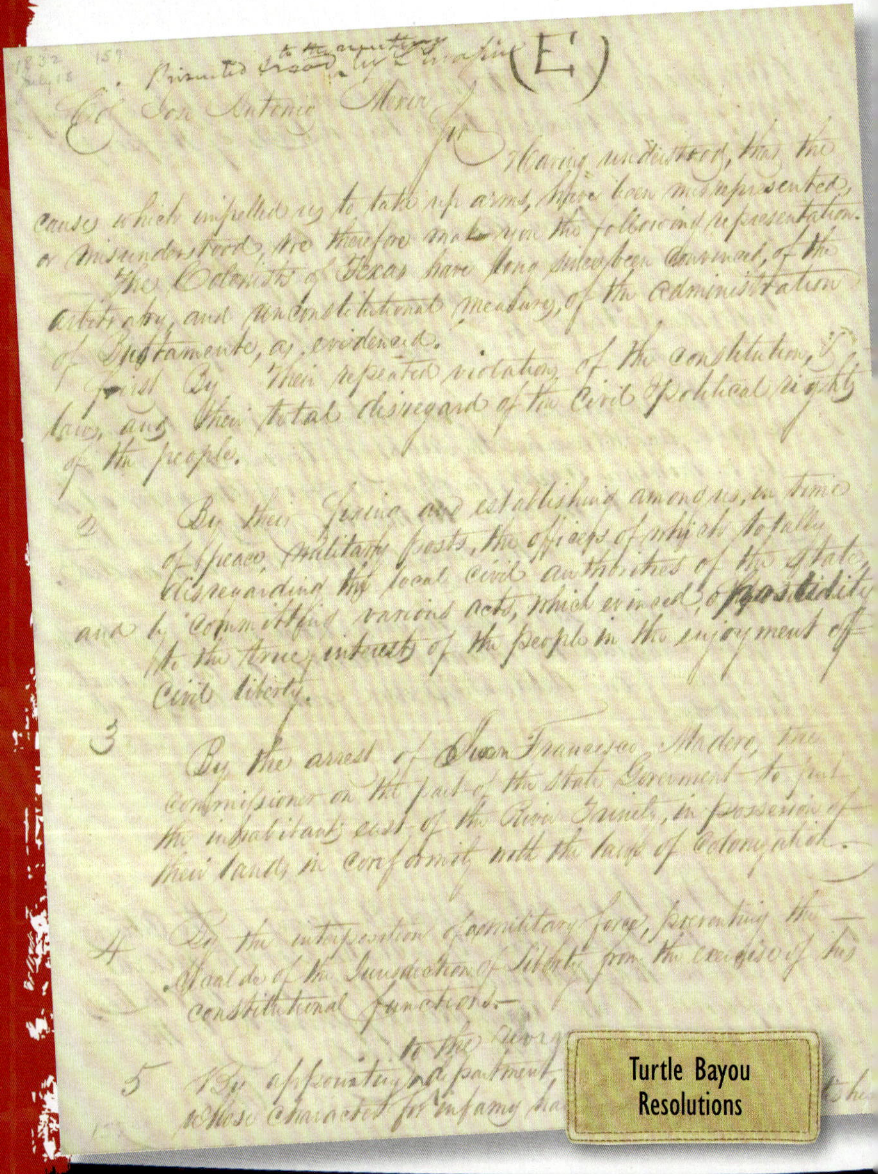

Turtle Bayou Resolutions

Revolution in Zacatecas

The Texas Revolution was not the only rebellion in the Mexican states. The **militia** (mi-LISH-uh) of Zacatecas (sah-kah-TE-kahs) rebelled against Santa Anna's government in 1835. Thousands of rebels were killed or taken prisoner. Santa Anna then marched north to regain control of Mexico.

Battle of Velasco

The Law of April 6, 1830 set up customs houses along Mexican waterways to collect **import** and **export** taxes. The taxes made the Texans angry. The Mexican government set up small military forts to provide armed support for the customs house. One fort, Velasco (beh LAHS-koh), was the scene of the first bloodshed of the Texas Revolution.

Mexico had other problems, too. In 1832, General Antonio López de Santa Anna tried to overthrow President Anastacio Bustamante. Santa Anna supported the **Constitution**, or set of laws, of 1824. So Texans were hopeful he would support them.

Antonio López de Santa Anna

At Turtle Bayou (BAHY-oo), Texans declared their support for Santa Anna. They wrote a document stating their complaints called the Turtle Bayou Resolutions. They said Bustamante had violated the constitution. They urged all Texans to support Santa Anna. He was elected president in 1833.

Austin went to Mexico City to meet with Mexican officials on behalf of Texans. He hoped Santa Anna would allow immigration from the United States to continue. He also wanted Santa Anna to grant Texas separate statehood from Coahulia. Santa Anna did not agree with Austin's ideas. While traveling back to Texas, Austin was arrested.

Santa Anna wanted absolute power over Mexico. He got rid of the Constitution of 1824. Santa Anna wanted his government to have more power and the Mexican states to have less power.

The Revolution Begins

The Battle of Gonzales

By 1835, rebellion had broken out across Mexico. Some Texans wanted to make peace with Santa Anna and the Mexican government, but others wanted to fight for their independence.

Santa Anna sent the Mexican Army to take control of Texas. But when Texans learned about the plan, they called a meeting. Officials were sent to Washington-on-the-Brazos to discuss their options. They could give in to Santa Anna or fight for their rights.

Before the Texans could make their plans, the Mexican Army marched toward San Antonio. They wanted to take back the cannon they had loaned to the town of Gonzales in 1831. The Mexican Army gathered across the Guadalupe River. Mexican Lieutenant Francisco Castañeda (frahn-SEES-coh cahs-tah-NYEH dah) called for the Texans to **surrender** the cannon.

Gonzales cannon that fired the first shot of the Texas Revolution

Texan volunteers at Gonzales

During the night, citizens of Gonzales sent out an alarm to other Texans asking for help. The Texans refused to surrender the cannon. The women of Gonzales drew a picture of a cannon on a white flag and wrote "Come and take it!"

The Texans attacked the Mexican Army. Without orders to engage in battle, Castañeda **retreated**. The events at Gonzales were an important turning point in the struggle for independence. Now the Texans knew that they would have to fight for their freedom.

The Texian Army

Texas did not have a professional army. The empresarios had provided protection for their colonists. When the Texas Revolution began, few men had any military training or experience. The fighting began so quickly that there was little time to raise and train an army. The Texans depended on volunteers to fight the Mexican Army.

Austin on Board

At first, Austin was not in favor of Texas independence. He wanted to repair the relationship with the Mexican government. But when the revolution began, he was ready to fight for Texas.

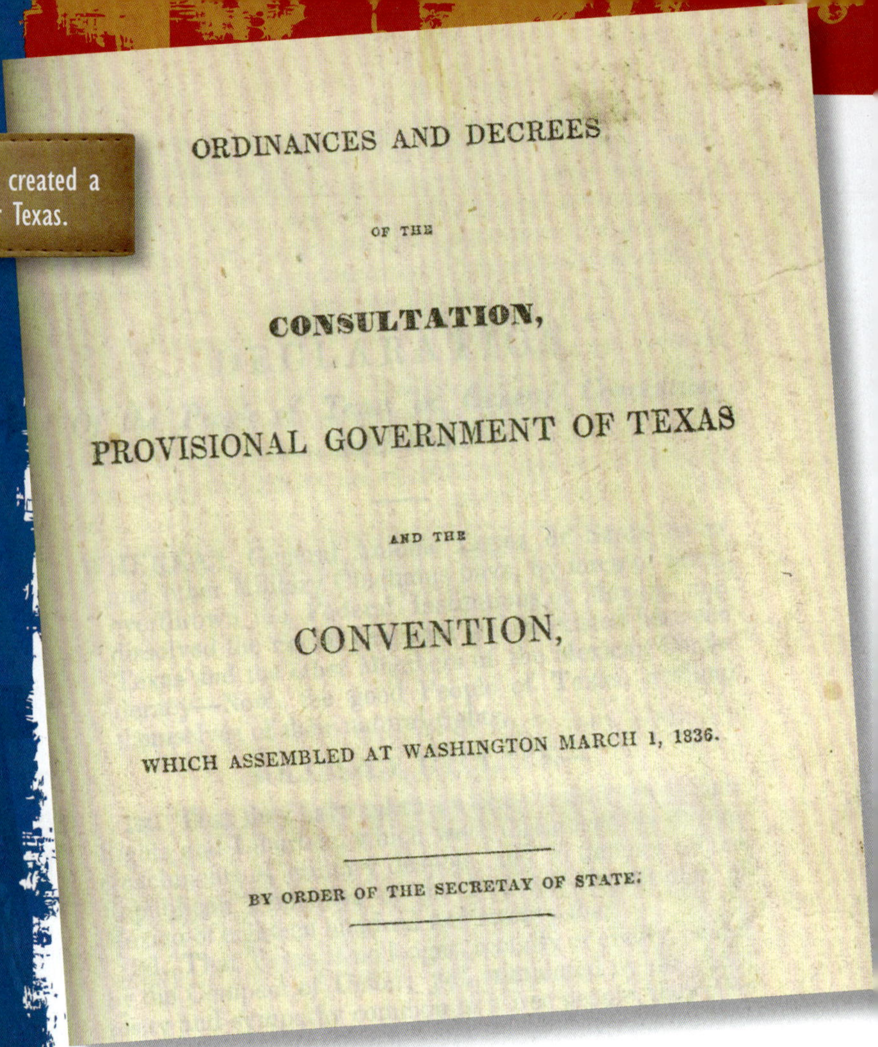
ORDINANCES AND DECREES

OF THE

CONSULTATION,

PROVISIONAL GOVERNMENT OF TEXAS

AND THE

CONVENTION,

WHICH ASSEMBLED AT WASHINGTON MARCH 1, 1836.

BY ORDER OF THE SECRETAY OF STATE.

"The Consultation" created a government for Texas.

The Consultation

On November 1, 1835, Texan leaders met together at what is called *the* ***Consultation***. The meeting was held at San Felipe (fuh-LEE-peh). **Delegates** discussed a new government for Texas. Some were longtime residents of Texas. Others had just arrived. They had different opinions about how to handle the situation with Mexico.

Attack on Matamoros

Some of the Texan leaders wanted to attack Mexico rather than simply defend their land in Texas. In December 1835, they planned to attack Matamoros (mat-uh-MAWR-uhs), a Mexican city on the Rio Grande River. With a victory, they hoped to win Mexican support. But the plan failed.

Sam Houston

As a boy, Sam Houston ran away from home and lived among the Cherokee (CHER-uh-kee). He joined the U.S. Army during the War of 1812. Houston studied law and was elected governor of Tennessee. But he resigned from office because of personal troubles. In 1832, Houston came to Texas looking for a fresh start.

Finally, the delegates issued a **declaration**. In it, they claimed that the people of Texas had a right to create their own independent government. It stated that the people of Texas would be loyal to Mexico if the government followed the Constitution of 1824. According to Austin, this was meant to win support among Texians and Tejanos for Texas independence.

The Consultation created a government for Texas. But it did not work well. There were many men who wanted power. Some Texans did not believe that Texians and Tejanos could work together.

The delegates had other problems, too. They needed an army. They also needed money and support from the United States. Sam Houston was appointed commander in chief of the Texian Army. Austin was sent to the United States to win support for Texas independence.

Sam Houston

The Siege of Bexar

By December 1835, the Texas town of Bexar (BEH-har), also known as San Antonio, was under the control of the Mexican Army. The Mexican forces numbered over 700 men, but there were only around 400 Texan volunteers.

The Texans had many problems. Most volunteers had no training as professional soldiers. Houston wanted to take time to train the men to fight, but Austin and others wanted to move forward. When Austin left to raise support from the United States, Edward Burleson (BUR-luh-suhn) was chosen to lead the volunteers.

This map shows the combat that took place near Mission Concepción.

Mission Concepción

On December 5, the Texans attacked Bexar. They dug trenches to connect the buildings they had captured. The fighting lasted four days. Then, Mexican General Martín Perfecto de Cos asked for a truce, or agreement, to stop fighting. Cos said the Texans could have San Antonio if he and his army were allowed to leave. The Mexican Army turned over most of their weapons to the Texans.

The **Siege** of Bexar was a victory for the Texans, but the fight for independence was far from over.

James Fannin

The Battle of Concepción

Austin sent James Fannin and James Bowie (BOH-ee) to the **Mission** Concepción (kohn-sep-SEEOHN). He wanted to know if the mission could serve as a military post. While they were there, General Cos attacked. In the Battle of Concepción, the Mexican army lost around 60 men and was forced to retreat.

The Grass Fight

In November 1835, Texans heard that Mexican troops were passing by carrying money to pay the Mexican Army. James Bowie led an attack on the troops. The Mexicans retreated and left their treasure behind. But what the Texans hoped were bags of silver were really bags of grass to feed horses.

The Alamo

The March Toward San Antonio

After the Siege of Bexar, Texan leaders were afraid the Mexican Army would attack San Antonio again.

Texans guarded the two main roads that led into Texas with forts. One fort, called *Presidio La Bahía* (preh-SEE-dyo lah bah-EE-ah), was at Goliad (GO-lee-ad). The other, in San Antonio, was an old Spanish mission known as *the Alamo*.

Major Green B. Jameson prepared for an attack on the Alamo. He had his men place cannons along the walls of the fort. The Alamo would provide the first defense against a Mexican attack.

In January 1836, James Clinton Neill, the leader of the Texan forces at Bexar, sent men to the Alamo as **reinforcements**. Houston thought the troops should be removed from the Alamo and that it should be torn down. Neill thought the Alamo would be easy to defend.

the Alamo

David Crockett

Reinforcements slowly arrived at the Alamo. Bowie came from Goliad on January 19. Lieutenant Colonel William B. Travis arrived with 30 **cavalrymen**. David Crockett brought 12 men with him on February 8.

Santa Anna marched toward San Antonio with more than 2,000 men armed with rifles, sabers, and cannons. The Texan men knew they were outnumbered. They only had around 150 men at the Alamo and 400 at Goliad.

James Bowie

David Crockett

Cheap land and opportunity for adventure drew many **frontiersmen** to Texas. Born in Tennessee, David Crockett served in the U.S. Congress and fought American Indians on the frontier. In 1836, he moved to Texas and joined the fight for independence.

Crockett was one of the most popular frontiersmen of his day. Stories about his life and adventures became even more legendary after his death. Though many of the stories are not true, Crockett is remembered by many as "king of the wild frontier."

Fall of the Alamo

In the middle of February 1836, Colonel Neill left the Alamo to care for his sick family. William Travis took his place in charge of the Alamo.

The Mexican army arrived on February 23. Santa Anna raised a red flag over the San Fernando Church, announcing that there would be no safe place for the Texans. Santa Anna wanted them to surrender, but Travis fired a cannon. This told Santa Anna that the Texans wanted to fight.

There were not enough men to defend the Alamo. Santa Anna launched cannon attacks on the fort for 13 days. Each night, under cover of darkness, the Mexican Army moved closer to the fort. The walls of the Alamo began to crumble.

Travis speaks to his men before the Battle of the Alamo.

defenders of the Alamo

On March 6, Santa Anna ordered his men to storm the fort. The Texans tried to defend themselves, but there were too many Mexican soldiers. Travis was one of the first men to die. Bowie died defending the Alamo, too.

All but seven of the men in the Alamo died in the attack. Santa Anna ordered these survivors to be shot. The Alamo had fallen, but Santa Anna had heavy losses, too. More than 600 Mexican soldiers died, weakening the Mexican Army for the rest of the war.

William Travis

"Victory or Death"

William Travis knew the men at the Alamo had no chance for survival unless help came from the outside. He sent several letters during the siege to raise support. In his final letter, Travis expressed his feelings clearly. He wrote, "I shall never surrender or retreat. . . Victory or Death."

Alamo Survivors

Although all of the fighting men were killed, there were several survivors at the Alamo. There were some 20 women, children, and slaves inside the fort during the attack. Susanna Dickinson was one of the survivors. She lived to tell the story of the Alamo.

Declaring Independence
The Republic of Texas

Texas leaders met at Washington-on-the-Brazos on March 1, 1836. They wanted to make plans for the future. Delegates from across Texas arrived to represent the interests of the people.

As the men arrived, they learned that the Alamo was under siege. Some wanted to march to the Alamo to help. But Houston persuaded them to stay and take care of important business.

On March 2, the delegates declared independence for Texas. They named Houston the commander of the army. As the Alamo fell, the Republic of Texas was born.

The Texas Constitution was similar to the U. S. Constitution. There was also a Declaration of Rights similar to the U. S. Bill of Rights. The Texas Constitution set strict limits on government officials. The president could serve only one three-year term. The Texas Constitution also protected slavery.

Washington-on-the-Brazos

David G. Burnet served as president until elections could be held. Lorenzo de Zavala (lo-REHN-soh deh sa-BAH-lah) was named vice president. Houston left to defend the new republic. The convention ended on March 17, 1836. But the revolution was not over.

David G. Burnet

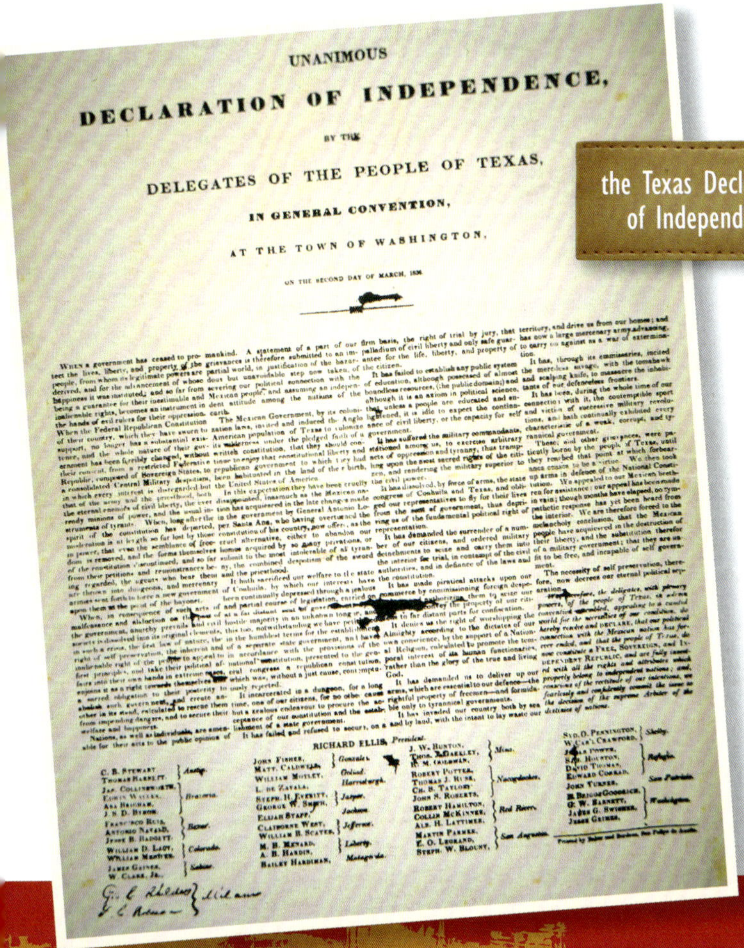

UNANIMOUS

DECLARATION OF INDEPENDENCE,

BY THE

DELEGATES OF THE PEOPLE OF TEXAS,

IN GENERAL CONVENTION,

AT THE TOWN OF WASHINGTON,

ON THE SECOND DAY OF MARCH, 1836.

RICHARD ELLIS, President.

the Texas Declaration of Independence

The Texas Declaration of Independence

When the meeting at Washington-on-the-Brazos got underway in March 1836, George Childress was there as a representative from Viesca (beeYES-kah), Mexico. Childress wrote the Texas Declaration of Independence. He wrote that Texas had a right to independence because the Mexican government had violated the constitution.

Lorenzo de Zavala

Zavala supported Texas independence in spite of being a native of Mexico. As a representative at the convention, he played an important role. Zavala helped write the constitution for the new Republic of Texas.

Sam Houston at San Jacinto

As the story of the Alamo spread, more volunteers arrived to help defend Texas. Santa Anna sent his forces across Texas to stop the rebellion.

Near Goliad, Mexican General Urrea (oo-REY-uh) captured Fannin and his troops. When news came that Fannin and around 350 men had been executed, Houston's men were furious.

On April 21, 1836, Houston and his men attacked Mexican soldiers while they slept near the San Jacinto (sahn ha-SEEN-toh) River. The Texian forces were joined by a group of Tejanos led by Juan Seguín (wahn seh-GEEN). Shouting "Remember the Alamo," they defeated Santa Anna's men. When the fighting was over, 600 Mexican soldiers lay dead and 700 more were taken prisoner. But only nine Texans died at the Battle of San Jacinto.

Houston and his men charge the Mexican army.

Santa Anna surrenders to Sam Houston.

Santa Anna managed to escape during the fighting. But he was captured the next day. Though his men wanted to execute Santa Anna, Houston decided to use him to end the fighting. Houston forced Santa Anna to sign an **armistice** (AHR-muh-stis), or agreement to stop fighting. This ended the Texas Revolution. The Texans had won the Battle of San Jacinto and secured independence for Texas.

The Runaway Scrape

After the fall of the Alamo, the people of Texas were frightened. They fled their homes, leaving everything behind. They wanted to escape the approaching Mexican army. This was called the *Runaway Scrape*.

Massacre at Goliad

When General Urrea captured Fannin and his men, they took them back to Goliad. Fannin thought they would be held as prisoners of war. Santa Anna ordered Urrea to execute all of the men. On March 27, the men were marched out of Goliad and shot. Fannin, already wounded, was killed inside the fort.

An Independent State

Obeying Santa Anna's orders, the Mexican Army withdrew from Texas. Although they had won their independence, the people of Texas faced many more challenges. There were still land disputes and political conflicts. Mexico did not recognize Texas's independence. The United States was unsure what relationship to have with Texas.

Even with these problems, many more people poured into Texas. Some Americans brought more slaves with them. More Mexicans came to live in Texas, too. Europeans, especially Germans, immigrated to Texas.

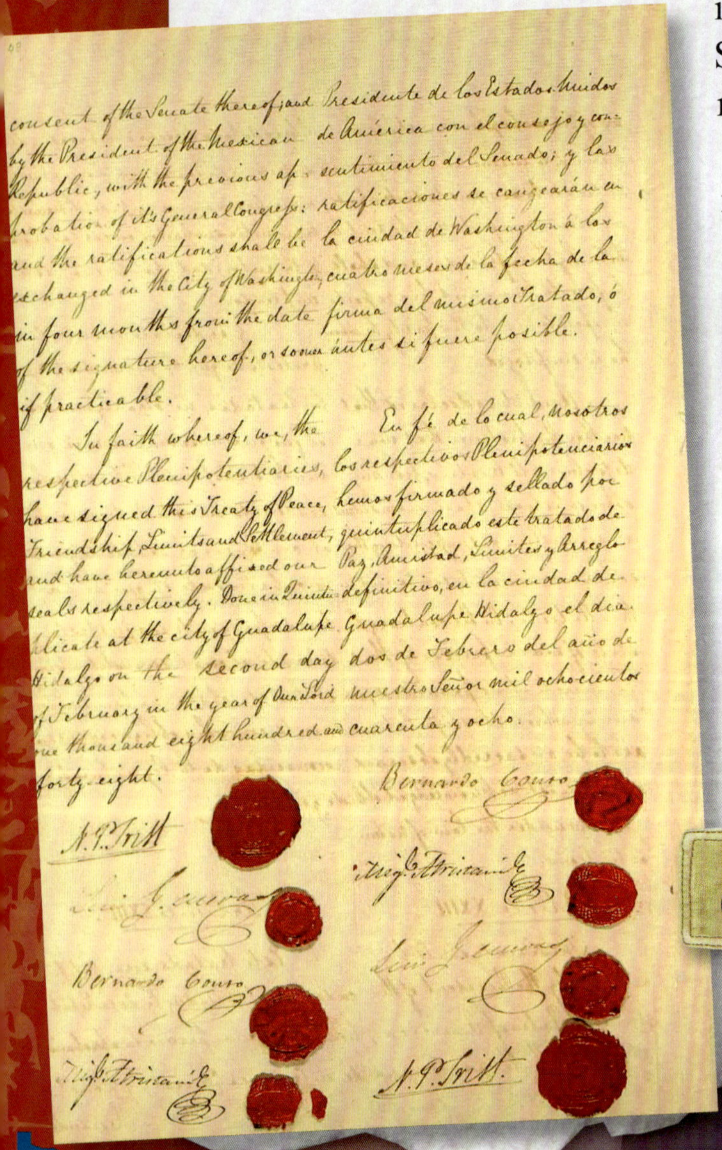
consent of the Senate thereof; and by the President of the Mexican Republic, with the previous approbation of its General Congress: and the ratifications shall be exchanged in the City of Washington in four months from the date of the signature hereof, or sooner if practicable.

In faith whereof, we, the respective Plenipotentiaries, have signed this Treaty of Peace, Friendship, Limits and Settlement, and have hereunto affixed our seals respectively. Done in Quintuplicate at the city of Guadalupe Hidalgo on the second day of February in the year of Our Lord one thousand eight hundred and forty-eight.

Presidente de los Estados Unidos de América con el consejo y consentimiento del Senado; y las ratificaciones se canjearán en la ciudad de Washington á los cuatro meses de la fecha de la firma del mismo tratado, ó antes si fuere posible.

En fé de lo cual, nosotros los respectivos Plenipotenciarios hemos firmado y sellado por quintuplicado este tratado de Paz, Amistad, Límites y Arreglo definitivo, en la ciudad de Guadalupe Hidalgo el día dos de Febrero del año de nuestro Señor mil ochocientos cuarenta y ocho.

N. P. Trist
Bernardo Couto

the Treaty of Guadalupe-Hidalgo

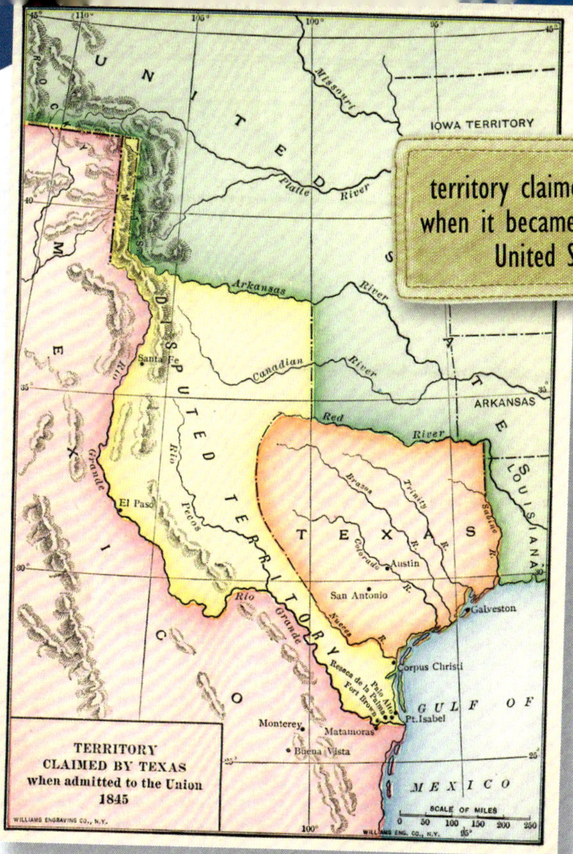

territory claimed by Texas when it became part of the United States

In 1845, Texas joined the United States. Soon, the United States and Mexico fought another war over Texas. The Mexican-American War ended in February 1848 with the Treaty of Guadalupe-Hidalgo. The Rio Grande was considered the new border between the two nations. Much territory that once was Mexico suddenly became part of the United States.

Texans still faced many problems. But they had greater control over their future. They had won the freedom to choose their own religion. And they had won the right to govern themselves.

President Houston

When the Texas Revolution ended, citizens elected a new government. Stephen F. Austin, Henry Smith, and Sam Houston all ran for the presidency. Houston was elected the first president of the Republic of Texas by a large number of votes.

Annexation

The first election was about more than forming a new government for Texas. Voters chose to adopt a constitution. They also voted in favor of **annexation** (an-ik-SEY-shuhn). Texans wanted independence, but they wanted protection, too. By joining the United States, they hoped to have the support of the U. S. Army in any future disputes with Mexico.

Glossary

annexation—to take over a territory and make it part of a larger territory

armistice—an agreement to stop fighting

cavalrymen—soldiers who fight on horseback

colonies—countries or areas under the control of another country; a group of people living there

constitution—a written statement outlining the basic laws for a state or country

consultation—a meeting for the purpose of making decisions

declaration—an announcement

delegates—people who represent other people at a meeting

empresarios—people given land grants by the Mexican government to make a settlement and recruit people to live there

export—to send goods out of a country or state

frontiersmen—people who live on the frontier

immigration—the act of moving to a new country

import—to bring goods into a country or state

inspection—the act of carefully looking over something

militia—a group of citizen soldiers

mission—a religious and military outpost established by the Spanish during colonization

plantation—a type of large farm found in the southern United States

provinces—districts or regions of a territory

rancher—a person who raises livestock such as cattle or horses

rebellion—open resistance to one's government

recruit—to select or get the services of someone

reinforcements—additional men used to build more strength

retreated—left a battlefield

revolution—an act of overthrowing and replacing one government with another

secede—to leave a country and form a new government

siege—a military strategy in which troops surround an area and cut off outside access to force a surrender

surrender—to give up

Tejanos—Mexican-born Texans

Texians—people living in Mexican Texas between 1821 and 1836

thriving—growing very well

transitions—the processes of changing from one form to another

Index

Alamo, 20–24, 26–27
Austin, Moses, 6–9
Austin, Stephen F., 13, 15, 17–19, 29
Battle of Concepción, 18–19
Battle of Gonzales, 14–15
Battle of San Jacinto, 26–27
Battle of Velasco, 12
Bowie, James, 19, 21, 23
Burleson, Edward, 18
Burnet, David G., 25
Bustamante, Anastacio, 13
Castañeda, Francisco, 14–15
Childress, George, 25
Constitution of 1824, 13, 17
Consultation, The, 16–17
Cos, General Martin Perfecto de, 19
Crockett, David, 21
De León, Martin, 7
Dickinson, Susanna, 23
Fannin, James, 19, 26–27
Goliad Massacre, 27
Grass Fight, 19
Guadalupe River, 14
Houston, Sam, 16–18, 20, 24–27, 29
Jameson, Green B., 20
Law of April 6, 1830, 10–12
Matamoros, Mexico, 16
Mexican-American War, 29
Mier y Terán, Manuel de, 10–11
Neill, James Clinton, 20, 22
Panic of 1819, 6–7
Plan of Iguala, 5
Presidio La Bahía, 20
Republic of Fredonia, 8
Republic of Texas, 4, 24–25, 29
Rio Grande River, 16, 29
Runaway Scrape, 27
San Jacinto River, 26
Santa Anna, Antonio López de, 5, 12–14, 21–23, 26–28
Siege of Bexar, 18–20
slavery, 9, 24
Travis, William B., 21–23
Treaty of Guadalupe-Hidalgo, 28–29
Turtle Bayou Resolutions, 12–13
Urrea, General Jose de, 26–27
Washington-on-the-Brazos, 14, 24–25
Zavala, Lorenzo de, 25

Your Turn!

In 1835, Mexican General Santa Anna sent soldiers to occupy Texas. He wanted to get the rebellious colonists under control. He ordered the Texans to give up their weapons. They refused. Mexican soldiers went to Gonzales to take back a cannon they had given the settlers. The settlers refused. Instead, they filled the cannon with scrap metal and fired it at the Mexican soldiers. This was the first battle of the Texas Revolution.

A Fitting Flag

Examine the Texian Army flag. Do you think the settlers chose a fitting design for their flag? Support your opinion with facts from the text.